A Walk in the
Town

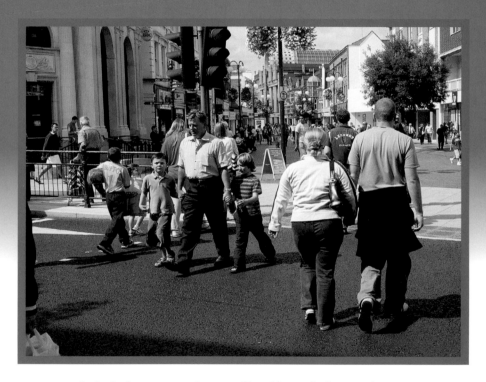

Written by Sally Hewitt
Photography by Chris Fairclough

FRANKLIN WATTS
LONDON•SYDNEY

Always go for a walk with an adult.

This edition 2012
published by Franklin Watts
338 Euston Road
London NW1 3BH

Franklin Watts Australia
Level 17 / 207 Kent Street
Sydney, NSW 2000

© Franklin Watts 2005

Editors: Caryn Jenner, Sarah Ridley
Designer: Louise Best
Art director: Jonathan Hair
Photography: Chris Fairclough
Map: Hardlines

The publisher wishes to thank Charles Welding
and Alexander and Andrew Somerville-Brown
for agreeing to be in this book.

A CIP catalogue record for this book is
available from the British Library

ISBN 978 1 4451 0761 5

Dewey decimal classification number: 307.76

Printed in China

Franklin Watts is a division of Hachette
Children's Books, an Hachette UK company.
www.hachette.co.uk

Contents

No traffic allowed

A town is busy with people and traffic.

Why is no traffic allowed on the main shopping street?

Street cleaning

The streets are kept clean.
There are litter bins for
people to put their rubbish.

The street cleaner's machine
washes the pavements and
sweeps up dirt and rubbish.

Inside and outside

This is the shopping centre.
Inside there are 86 shops
and restaurants.

Outside, you walk along pavements and cross roads to get to the shops. Do you like shopping in a shopping centre, or at shops on the street?

Market place

Follow the sign to the market place. Do you think the merry-go-round is always there?

This market stall sells fresh food.
The fruit and vegetables look
and smell delicious!

Bridge over the river

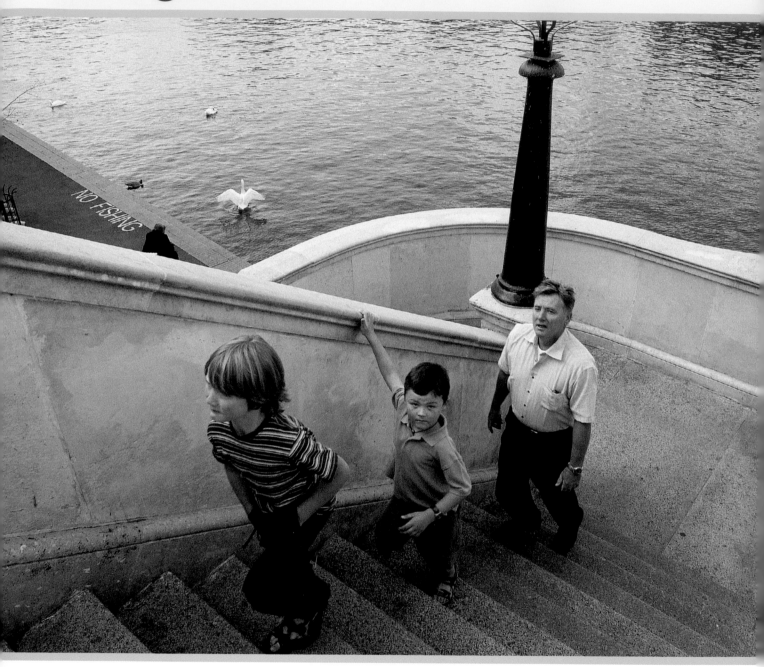

A bridge crosses the river that flows through the town. Steps take you down to the riverside - and up again!

There is a footpath, a cycle track
and a road over the bridge.

Money to spend

A big bank stands in
the town centre.

You don't have to go inside to get out some money.

Crossing the road

Traffic stops while people cross the road at the pedestrian crossing.

What tells the traffic to stop?

A bus full of people stops
at the crossing. They might be
coming to shop in the town, or
just be passing through.

Old and new

Old and new buildings stand side by side.
An old building contains a new shop.

A big new cinema can show
14 different films at once.

Look up!

Look up! What can you see above the busy street? A church clock and old street lamps.

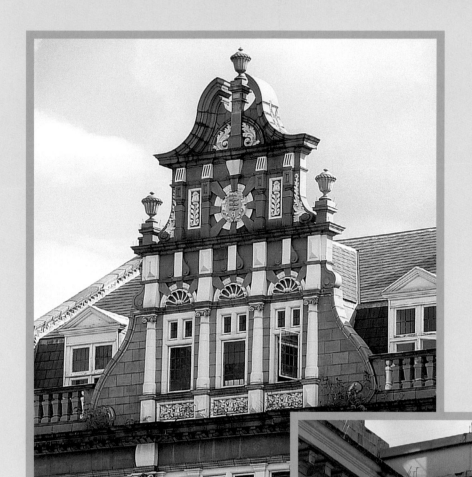

Patterns and ornaments on top of buildings.

A golden statue and a lion's head.

What else might you see?

Going home

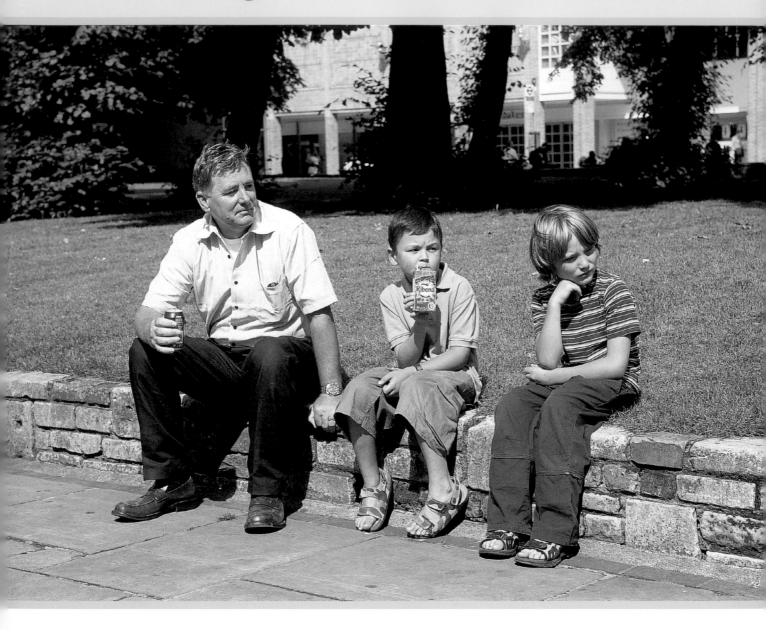

A little park is a quiet place to rest after a busy day in the town.
Now it's time to go home.

A timetable tells you the time your train leaves. What other ways could you get home?

Map

You can start a walk from any point on a map. To follow the walk in this book, put your finger on **Start** and trace the route.

Key

pedestrian area

bench

shopping centre

market place

bridge

bank

cinema

park

church

bus stop

railway station

parking

Quiz

It's important to keep the town clean. How are the streets kept clean?

Look at pages 8 and 9.

There are fruit and vegetable stalls in the market place.
What else is in the market place?

Look at pages 12 and 13.

A river flows through the town. How can you cross the river?

Look at page 15.

A bank stands on the
main street.
What other buildings
are there in the town?

Look all through the book.

The roads are busy with
traffic.
How can you cross the
road safely?

Look at pages 18 and 19.

You can rest in a little park.
Where else can you sit and
rest in the town?

Look all through the book.

Index